⊞ NOTHING SEEN IN MY WORK BY ANYONE IS TAKEN FROM ANYTHING, ANYWHERE. SO AS THEY SAY IN THE MOVIES "ALL RESEMBLANCES TO BUILDINGS LIVING OR DEAD IS PURELY COINCIDENTAL AND NOT INTENDED BY ME." ⊞

—FRANK LLOYD WRIGHT
\ "INFLUENCE OR RESEMBLANCE," 1953

FRANK LLOYD WRIGHT'S
FIRST HOUSES

CARLA LIND

AN ARCHETYPE PRESS BOOK
POMEGRANATE ARTBOOKS, SAN FRANCISCO

© 1996 Archetype Press, Inc.

Text © 1996 Carla Lind

Library of Congress Cataloging-in-Publication Data

Lind, Carla.

Frank Lloyd Wright's First houses / Carla Lind.

  p.   cm.   — (Wright at a glance)

"An Archetype Press book."

Includes bibliographical references.

ISBN 0-7649-0014-5 (hc)

1. Dwellings — Middle West. 2. Prairie school (Architecture). 3. Wright, Frank Lloyd, 1867–1959 — Criticism and interpretation. I. Title. II. Series: Lind, Carla. Wright at a glance.

NA7218.L55 1996   96-18141

728'.372'092—dc20   CIP

Published by

Pomegranate Artbooks

Box 6099, Rohnert Park,

California 94927-6099

Catalogue no. A859

Produced by Archetype Press, Inc.

Washington, D.C.

Project Director: Diane Maddex

Editorial Assistants:

Gretchen Smith Mui and Kristi Flis

Designer: Robert L. Wiser

10 9 8 7 6 5 4 3 2 1

Printed in Singapore

Opening photographs:

Page 1: Frank Lloyd Wright about 1887. Page 2: Heller house (1896), Chicago. Pages 6–7: Winslow house (1893), River Forest, Illinois.

CONTENTS

N

O GREAT ARTIST SIMPLY APPEARS one morning fully blossomed. Instead, genius is usually cajoled from within by powerful outside forces and then revealed after years of absorbing, shaping, evolving, and experimenting. Frank Lloyd Wright (1867–1959) was no exception. He was groomed to be an architect from his earliest childhood—first by his family, then by society, and finally by his employers. He was influenced by what he was taught, what he read, what he heard, and, most important, what he saw.

Wright acknowledged the pivotal roles of five forces on his seventy-year architectural career: his lifelong teacher, nature; the Unitarianism of his family; his education in the Froebel system, which combined geometry and botany; the simplicity and modularity of Japanese design; and the architect Louis Sullivan. Wright did not own up to other influential factors, identified by scholars for decades, such as the Arts and Crafts, Vienna Secession, and modern design movements. There is no doubt that his awareness of rival contemporary architecture as well

The Moore house of 1895 in Wright's hometown of Oak Park illustrates a dilemma of the architect's early years: his clients wanted a traditional home—in this case Eliza-bethan—while Wright was eager to try out his own ideas of organic architecture.

as historical precedents also served to sharpen his skills as a designer.

Wright's transition from a young student and apprentice to a world-renowned architect was measured. Fortunate to begin his practice near the turn of the twentieth century—when all America was seeking change—he was surrounded by innovations. Increased mechanization and availability of goods and rapid growth were brought on by the industrial age and expanded railways. Arriving in Chicago from his home in Wisconsin in 1887, just sixteen years after the devastating Chicago fire, he found himself in the middle of a building boom.

Wright was in search of work, having completed less than a year of engineering at the University of Wisconsin. His commissions began while he was still apprenticing to his first employer, Joseph Lyman Silsbee. Like ripples from a rock tossed into a pond, they grew in concentric circles that radiated from his family, friends, business associates, and neighbors. His earliest clients were his aunts, who asked him to design their Hillside Home School (1887) in Spring Green, Wisconsin.

▓ As would have any other youngster fresh from the hinterland, however gifted, Wright arrived unformed as an architect, and it was to take him nearly a decade and a half to find his own manner. These years constituted the "long foreground." ▓

James O'Gorman
Three American Architects, 1991

Oak Park residents, even clients of Wright, were fond of the Queen Anne style. His 1893 design for the Walter Gales paid homage to this Victorian style but transformed it with simplified geometric volumes and details.

Rev. Jenkin Lloyd Jones, his uncle, led the popular All Souls Church, through which Wright met many of his earliest Chicago clients. Later contacts in the office of Adler and Sullivan led to more of his first commissions. Word of his talent spread rapidly, so that by 1900 he was well known in the Chicago area and had developed his theories of organic architecture.

Wright's most popular expression of that design philosophy became the Prairie Style house, but this was preceded by thirteen years of experimentation and a determined effort to set himself apart from other architects. In the fifty buildings that Wright completed during his developmental years from 1887 to 1900, his personal architectural approach took shape. In his first houses Wright demonstrated his ability to master historic styles, yet he gradually gained enough confidence to persuade his clients to break with convention in small ways and then in larger schemes until his architectural vision was clear. His revolution began on the inside, as Wright opened up formal spaces and incorporated simple, well-crafted features to enhance livability.

One of the houses that Wright remodeled was the residence of the H. P. Young family of Oak Park. For this 1895 makeover the architect changed the interior from Victorian to Wrightian with wood screens and banding that tied together diverse spaces.

APPRENTICESHIPS

JOSEPH LYMAN SILSBEE

THE YOUNG ARCHITECT'S FIRST EMPLOYER

THE TWENTY-YEAR-OLD WRIGHT arrived in Chicago in early 1887 looking for a job. He was soon hired by Joseph Lyman Silsbee, a fellow Unitarian who had migrated to the Midwest two years earlier. Silsbee had been commissioned by Wright's uncle to design his large church (1886) in Chicago and a small family church in Wisconsin, Unity Chapel (1886), which Wright had helped supervise. During the six months Wright spent as his draftsman, Silsbee aided Wright with his design for his aunts' Hillside Home School and some other proposed houses for family lands nearby.

Silsbee was adept at the popular Shingle Style, an informal, asymmetrical, and picturesque mode. Signature features—complex steep roofs and gables, polygonal bays and turrets, broad sash windows, wooden shingle skins over late Victorian forms, and generous porches—all worked their way into Wright's earliest designs. Interior spaces became more fluid, less compartmentalized, and ornament was restrained. Although it was based on historic forms, the style allowed for considerable inventiveness and introduced Wright to domestic planning.

His early and perpetual fascination with residential architecture had several sources. J. L. Silsbee's encouragement and Louis Sullivan's decision to turn his few house commissions over to Wright may have awakened an interest compounded by later successes.

Robert C. Twombly
Frank Lloyd Wright:
An Interpretive Biography, 1973

The Shingle Style was so appealing to Wright that he used it for his own first home (1889) in Oak Park. He made the style his own in part by grouping windows to create screens bringing light inside.

LOUIS SULLIVAN

WRIGHT'S LIEBER MEISTER

> ▪▪ Yes, the significant implication of lieber-meister's gift to me was his practice "of-the-thing-not-on-it" which I recognized and saw most clearly realized in his unique sense of ornament. ▪▪
>
> **Frank Lloyd Wright**
> "Genius and the Mobocracy,"
> 1949

Among the houses that Wright claimed to have designed while employed by Adler and Sullivan was a rowhouse (1892) in Chicago for Sullivan's mother, Adrienne. The extent of Wright's involvement in the design of the house, now demolished, is not certain.

WRIGHT'S ARCHITECTURAL PRINCIPLES solidified under the tutelage of Louis Sullivan from 1888 to 1893. Working at the side of this rebellious theoretician, whom Wright called his *lieber Meister* (beloved teacher), he became schooled in the need for an indigenous American architecture. Sullivan was the spiritual leader of the Chicago School, an original response to the proliferation of historically derived styles. While Wright would soon decry copies of historic styles, his early domestic designs in fact explored various eclectic forms of the day.

Wright was an eager learner at Adler and Sullivan and was given great responsibility, particularly for residential commissions. As chief draftsman, Wright gained considerable expertise in engineering as well as in the use of integral ornament. Sullivan's masterful ornamental style found its source in nature but was combined with mathematical precision. Called conventionalization, each of his nature-based geometric interpretations was an original. Wright absorbed what he saw and heard, adopting Sullivan's theories but developing his own simplified style of ornament.

THE YEAR AFTER SULLIVAN ASSIGNED Wright to design vacation homes for both Sullivan and his friend James Charnley in Mississippi, he called on the young architect to help with Charnley's city house. Wright's design for the massive $25,000 house was radically simple for the time. Now home to the Society of Architectural Historians, it was elegantly restrained on the exterior, turning inward for privacy and repose.

The crisp, symmetrical facade is anchored by a large, smooth stone base below narrow Roman brick walls and a flat roof. With horizontal lines and geometric purity, he conveyed the house's simple function. Although the design was generally not derivative, art glass around the front door has a traditional medieval pattern and the overall design recalls a Renaissance town house.

The plan is as simple as the three-part facade indicates: a stairway in the center, with a large room on each side. Strong Richardsonian arches mark the openings on the main floor, which are counterpoints to the dominant rectilinear themes. Here Wright clearly demonstrated his ability to portray dignity without pretension.

Limited Sullivanesque ornament appears on the front balcony (opposite). Inside, richly carved wood in Sullivanesque patterns tops newel posts (above), creates a delicate spindled screen with fretwork panels (page 20), and frames the arched entry hall on the first floor (page 21).

McARTHUR HOUSE

CHICAGO, ILLINOIS. 1892

▫▫ After the realization of the Prairie house around 1900, Wright was quick to dismiss all architectural historicism as mere "sentimentality." Yet his own work from 1887–1893 shows considerable derivation from historic styles and from current trends in American architecture. ▫▫

Jack Quinan
In *Frank Lloyd Wright:
In the Realm of Ideas,* 1988

The McArthur house incorporated a few features that Wright may have picked up from his work with Sullivan, such as an open arcade surrounding the front porch.

WRIGHT SOUGHT TO ALLEVIATE SOME of his financial needs by doing a few residential designs after hours—a violation of his contract with Adler and Sullivan. To avoid being detected, he listed his friend Cecil Corwin as the architect of several. Each of the six or seven "bootleg" designs manipulates a historic style.

Wright provided the McArthurs with a variation on a Dutch colonial, including a gambrel roof, dormers, polygonal bays, and walls of Roman brick below stucco. Bays beneath the eaves at the corners, an unconventional detail, helped release the space. Leaded glass windows on the main floor were in a diamond design, like a pattern Wright used in his own 1889 home.

After a 1902 remodeling the dining room was praised for its "softness without dimness, warmth without stuffiness, simplicity without bareness, and plenty of light with no suggestion of either garishness or glare." A built-in oak sideboard had geometric art glass doors and elaborate woodwork incorporating Wright's signature banding. Burlap in soft gold covered the frieze and ceiling of the golden room.

BLOSSOM HOUSE

NEXT DOOR TO THE McARTHURS, Wright designed for the Blossom family a gracious New England colonial, complete with Ionic columns, Palladian windows, and a portico. It was another "bootleg" job.

As with many of his early houses, the fireplace is faced with rectangular glazed tiles. It is nestled into a cozy inglenook with a wooden cupboard above and serves as the living room's central feature. Horizontal wood panels separated by tiny beads wrap around the living room up to shoulder height, creating an embracing horizontal envelope. The south side of the room leads to a small terrace, releasing the space. A semicircular conservatory likewise opens the dining room to the back yard, as in the Winslow house of the following year. Arched doorways repeat the curved form.

Wood spindles, simply turned, create a screen between the living room and the stairhall. The large house has five bedrooms at the top of a broad staircase. Art glass in the upper stairhall incorporates conventional festoons with diamond-patterned panes—falling short of the geometric purity of Wright's later designs.

■■ There could be on Wright's part at this time, as never again, an actual choice between possible "styles," motivated by the desire to avoid in his private work the manner associated with Sullivan. ■■

Henry-Russell Hitchcock
In the Nature of Materials, 1942

Similar to a plan published by the classical architects McKim, Mead and White, the Blossom facade is symmetrical and formal, but Wright added unique features on the interior to leave his mark.

CLARK HOUSE

LA GRANGE, ILLINOIS · 1892

THE CLARK HOUSE WAS NOT TRACED to Wright until 1967, when drawings for it were found in a loft at Taliesin. Although it had been attributed to him in 1894, Wright later suggested that it was designed by E. H. Turnock. The house certainly fits into Wright's stylistic repertoire of the time. An early architect's lien on the house indicates that the relationship between Wright and the owner-contractor was acrimonious.

Three stories high, the house is clad in clapboard with a beaded edge. Wright's drawings indicate that it was intended to be a modified English Tudor with thin, vertical strips applied to stucco walls on the upper stories, much like the Moore house (1895), but only the back wall was built this way and then covered with clapboard like the others before it was completed.

Few Wright innovations are visible in the center-hall plan, which has conventional drawing, reception, and sitting rooms. The four fireplaces have wood mantels with simple geometric details and glazed tile fronts. Circular patterns in the art glass recall several other Wright houses of the time and predate his rectilinear forms.

❝ He was indeed the Great Emancipator of architecture, but this is largely because he was one of its greatest assimilators. ❞

William Marlin
American Heritage, 1981

Although grander, the Clark house shares many features with Wright's own 1889 home in Oak Park: cross-gabled roofs, dual polygonal bays in front, a modified Palladian window beneath the gable, and Shingle Style forms.

WALTER GALE HOUSE

OAK PARK, ILLINOIS, 1893

NOT FAR FROM HIS OWN HOME, Wright designed three houses for his friends the Gales, a prominent local family who were among Wright's most loyal patrons. Two of the houses were part of the "bootleg" designs commissioned by the realtor Thomas Gale, one of which he sold to Robert Parker. The third, for Thomas's pharmacist brother, Walter, was designed after Wright opened his own office.

Along with Wright's Emmond house (1892) in La Grange, all three shared the same architectural grammar. Wright used the Queen Anne style but reformulated its elements. The steep gabled roofs and tall chimneys are typical, but Wright wrapped the turrets and bays with ribbons of windows, created more boldly geometric masses, and opened and simplified interior spaces.

The restrained spindled balustrade of the broad entry porch reappears in the beautifully articulated stairhall. Horizontal wood paneling alternating with delicate beadwork clothes the entrance, while wood banding and low ceilings suggest a human scale, unlike the tall Victorian parlors more characteristic of the period.

▓ Intent on proving the greatness of his soul from an early age, Wright cherished his inconsistencies as if they were among his most beloved creations. ▓

William Cronin
Frank Lloyd Wright: Architect,
1994

Here the semicircle replaced the octagon as Wright's dominant sculptural form for the facade. It is a more original expression than his other Queen Annes, yet a small classical swag remains below the dormer window—a gesture to the tastes of the day.

WINSLOW HOUSE

RIVER FOREST, ILLINOIS, 1893

BOTH WRIGHT AND SULLIVAN denounced the classicism that dominated the World's Columbian Exposition in Chicago in 1893, the year Wright opened his practice. The Winslow house embodies Wright's struggle to reconcile this popular style with what he had learned from Sullivan. It was a pivotal step in his odyssey toward an original architectural statement.

Wright's desire to simplify the features of a house shows in the symmetrical street facade of golden brick, stone, and plaster. Restraint breaks loose on the back, where an informal, asymmetrical massing was dictated by interior spaces. The generous entrance hall has a classical arcade raised on a platform in front of the fireplace. A large curved conservatory enables the dining room to abandon the confines of standard boxy rooms.

William Winslow was an ornamental iron specialist and printer whose Auvergne Press was housed in the carriage house Wright also designed. His wooded lot featured a large elm that became a metaphor for the house, with its defined base, rising trunk, leafy cornice, and broad, sheltering roof.

:: The Winslow house had burst on the view of that provincial suburb like a Prima Vera in full bloom.... That house became an attraction, far and near. Incessantly it was courted and admired. Ridiculed, too, of course. ::

Frank Lloyd Wright
An Autobiography, 1932

The foliage-based sculptural ornament of the wide plaster frieze pays homage to Louis Sullivan, as does the band of carved stone that unifies the door and window unit—much like Sullivan's **Wainwright tomb** (1892) in Chicago.

WILLIAMS HOUSE

RIVER FOREST, ILLINOIS. 1895

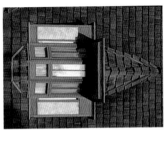

THE HOUSE WRIGHT DESIGNED FOR his Wisconsin friends the Chauncey Williamses was yet another experiment in originality. Described as medieval, Gothic, and Japanese, it derived from both Silsbee and Sullivan. The exaggeratedly steep roof, shallow base, and strong, rustic foundation are unique in Wright's portfolio.

Heavy wood moldings delineate the openings, define the base's horizontality, and confirm its embrace of the earth. Sullivanesque wood fretwork surrounds an arched doorway. A Gothic window adjoins the entry, while medieval oriel-like dormers added five years later pierce the roof. Octagonal forms creating bays in the front turret and side continue Wright's efforts to eliminate boring rooms in favor of looser, more open spaces with generous amounts of windows. The plan, unlike others of the period, placed the living room in the back of the house, where it opens to a garden.

Williams became a partner with Wright and Winslow in publishing William C. Gannett's *The House Beautiful*. Like the Williams house, the book juxtaposes geometry with nature, a continuous theme of Wright's.

Symbolizing an architecture drawn from the earth, boulders for the house were gathered from the nearby Des Plaines River by the Wrights, Winslows, and Williamses. Above the irregular base rise crisp forms of brick and stucco.

MOORE HOUSE

OAK PARK, ILLINOIS · 1895

THE ATTORNEY NATHAN MOORE FIRST considered remodeling an older house, but his wife, Anna, wanted something more Elizabethan. Reconciling Wright's own desire to be original with his clients' request yielded another artful interpretation of a historic style. He proved proficient in the details of English Tudor, but Wright deviated by adding an open porch, elaborated on the traditional interior paneling, and used his delicate spindled screens. Beneath its steeply pitched roof with half-timbering on each end, the three-story house had a large ballroom.

The dramatic siting to the far north edge of the large lot provided a sunny garden as well as southern light for the house. Wright continued to use this technique frequently in his Prairie houses of the next decade.

The top half of the house was lost in a Christmas fire in 1922. Wright, who had also designed the Moores' pergola and garden pavilion in 1905, was called back to redo the top part of the damaged house. Wright's repair produced a more stylized Tudor that incorporated some of the Mayan ornament he then favored.

In its original incarnation (opposite), the Moore house proclaimed its medieval origins in half-timbered gables. A band of diamond-paned windows helped lighten the clublike interior. Wright expanded the Tudor vocabulary with his own touches (above).

With these forced tributes to tradition, which have in themselves a certain undeniable charm, there is not only an admirable directness and simplicity of plan shown here but a breadth and symmetry of massing and composition as well.

Robert Spencer
Architectural Review, 1900

The house as redesigned after the 1922 fire was not as tall as the original but drew together the chimneys into one integral design feature. Only the ends of the house retained some half-timbering. Its exotic sculptural forms recall other Wright projects of the 1920s.

THE OAK PARK INVENTOR AND BUSINESSMAN Charles Roberts commissioned Wright to design a house (1892), residential development (1896), grandfather clock, summer cottage (1896), and quadruple block (1897)—none of which was built. He was the link to Wright's commissions for Mrs. Roberts's sister Anna Bradley (1900) and brother Warren Hickox (1900). Like Wright, Roberts was the son of a Unitarian minister and loved music. As chairman of the building committee for Unity Temple (1904), he played a major role in the success of Wright's design.

Roberts did succeed in having Wright remodel his large 1886 house by Burnham and Root. The new design changed roof details, the central stairhall, and the rear southwest corner and featured Wright's masterful wood trim. Oak stringcourses reduced the scale of the house and tied together all elements. A fold-away bed was built into the wall to create a downstairs bedroom. The living room fireplace, with fret-paneled oak doors on the mantel cupboard, demonstrated Wright's ability to translate Sullivan's ornamental designs into more geometric, modular forms that were his own.

The entrance hall (opposite) was outfitted with built-in seating, paneled with horizontal beadwork boards, and led to rhythmic rows of slender spindles that defined the rising stairs. A pastoral mural by Pauline Dohn dissolved the lower stair wall.

The bold yet delicately pierced doors of the mantel cupboard create an optical illusion when open. Mirrors inside reflect light out—magically giving the appearance of a more elaborate box within.

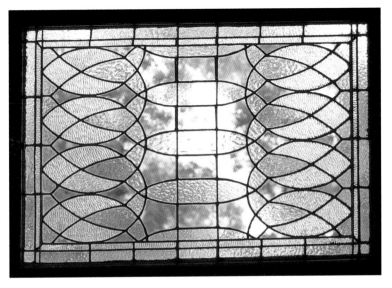

Wright's designs for the Roberts house glass were simple, clear, and curvilinear. A large flowerlike arch of art glass in the stairhall (opposite) opens the wall at the top of the stairs. Like petals, the overlapping segments of circles fan out from the center. The floral motif extended to the study windows nearby (left).

⊞ Then came the period of transition, when he was trying to break away from Sullivanism, casting about for methods of self-expression. ⊞

Apprentice Charles E. White
Letter, 1904

HELLER HOUSE

CHICAGO, ILLINOIS. 1896

DESIGNED FOR A NARROW CITY LOT, this house, like the Husser (1899, demolished) and Rollin Furbeck (1897) commissions, exalted clean, rectangular forms generously appointed with Sullivanesque ornament.

An elaborate terra-cotta frieze beneath the higher of two hipped roofs (see page 2) was modeled by Richard Bock, who shaped rows of sensuous dancing figures amid luscious vegetation. Wright used open arcades, colonnades, and rows of deep-set windows to relieve the tall Roman brick walls of their solidity.

Inside, Wright made a major leap into more spacious and articulated spaces. The indirect side entrance opens to a hall leading to the living room in one direction and the dining room in the other. Both pushed their boundaries, creating cruciform shapes seen frequently in the next decade. For unity with the warm golds of the oak, Wright called for a color scheme of dull green and bronze tones. The long, low fireplace and built-in sideboard cabinet with geometric art glass doors are richly styled and proportioned, emphasizing the horizontality—thus the domesticity and repose—of the interiors.

Stylized floral ornament surrounds the front door and outlines the panels beneath the windows. The house has a smaller, hipped-roof third story above a larger, lower hipped roof. Its crown is a monumental frieze, a panel of which Wright hung in his own Oak Park studio.

Wright designed some of his earliest furniture for the Heller house, but it is not known how much of it was made. Only a few built-in elements remain, such as this dining room cabinet featuring octagonal colonettes, a prototype for a motif used elsewhere in the house.

GEORGE FURBECK HOUSE

OAK PARK, ILLINOIS, 1897

WRIGHT'S FASCINATION WITH THE octagon was at its highest point during his early years. He used partial octagons for turrets and bays in numerous houses and as a detached form for his own studio (1898). For George and Susan Furbeck, however, it was the central form of their house and effectively broke open the box that Wright so disliked.

Two octagonal turrets housing a library and staircase flank a central octagonal living room. Intersecting each other, then joining with other rectangular elements, they are accented with triangular and square decorative elements and then topped with a cone-shaped roof. The octagon became the foundation of a playful geometric spree. Colorful brick and double rows of tiny dentils add to the exterior's checkered texture.

Detailing inside continues to dissolve the walls: geometric art glass doors fold open, the ceiling appears to float above linear molding, mirrored panels are built into the fireplace wall, spindled screens replace walls, and built-in furniture becomes part of the house. Wright made a giant leap toward an original architecture.

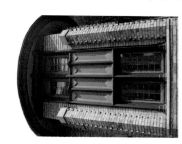

Custom masonry called for alternating the greenish ends and peach-toned stretchers of the common brick (above and opposite). In the house, wood defines the dining room (page 50), while translucent art glass helps eliminate the solidity of standard walls (page 51).

ROLLIN FURBECK HOUSE

OAK PARK, ILLINOIS, 1897

WRIGHT'S TRANSITION TO THE PRAIRIE Style is evident in the house he designed for George Furbeck's brother Rollin. Its geometric massing and sheltering, hipped roofs anticipated the next decade, yet Wright also interpreted classical ornament here in his own way.

Fluted octagonal columns with capitals in a stylized leaf pattern mark the second and third stories of the central three-story tower. Simple integral ornament comes from brickwork such as corbeling and projecting bands. The square plan is extended to the south with a porte-cochère (now enclosed) and to the east with an entry porch. On the west side, a third-floor balcony was cantilevered over a lower porch, later incorporated into the house to enlarge the dining room and kitchen.

The living room features two new elements: a large picture window and a preformed concrete fireplace and inglenook. Panels of diagonally paned art glass framed in pale gold were inset into the top section of most other windows. Here Wright's ability to contrast openness with intimate alcoves—to convey both spaciousness and protective shelter—was taking shape.

■■ Diverse in form, purpose and expression, there is a quality of style in **Mr. Wright's works which, even to the unschooled eye of the layman, stamps it as his, and which relates all to the others.** ■■

Robert Spencer

Architectural Review, 1900

The spindled wood screen that became a **Wright** trademark reappeared here to open up the stairway. More wood outlines a ledge and wall, leading the eye through the house. Art glass in a simple diamond pattern resembles the glass in his own Oak Park home, designed nearly a decade earlier.

Salmon-colored brick changes to stucco with wood trim above the sill of the second-story windows, creating another horizontal line to reduce the house's perceived height. An open dentil ribbon surrounds the exterior beneath the roof soffits.

Brooks, H. Allen, ed. *Writings on Wright.* Cambridge: MIT
 Press, 1981.

Gill, Brendan. *Many Masks: A Life of Frank Lloyd Wright.*
 New York: G. P. Putnam's Sons, 1987.

Hitchcock, Henry-Russell. *In the Nature of Materials.* 1942.
 Reprint. New York: Da Capo Press, 1975.

Manson, Grant Carpenter. *Frank Lloyd Wright to 1910: The
 First Golden Age.* New York: Van Nostrand Rein-
 hold, 1958.

O'Gorman, James F. *Three American Architects: Richardson,
 Sullivan and Wright.* Chicago: University of Chicago
 Press, 1991.

Pfeiffer, Bruce Brooks, ed. *Frank Lloyd Wright: Monographs.
 1887–1901.* Vol. I. Tokyo: ADA Edita. 1986.

Riley, Terence, ed. *Frank Lloyd Wright: Architect.* New
 York: Museum of Modern Art, 1994.

Twombly, Robert C. *Frank Lloyd Wright: An Interpretive
 Biography.* New York: Harper and Row, 1973.

Wright, Frank Lloyd. *Frank Lloyd Wright: Collected Writings.*
 Vols. I–5. Edited by Bruce Brooks Pfeiffer. New
 York: Rizzoli, 1992–95.

The author wishes to thank
Audrey and James Kouvel,
James and Mary Leatherberry,
Lars and Mary Lofgren,
Linda and William Ryan,
and John Thorpe for their
assistance.

Illustration Sources:

© Judith Bromley: 2, 15,
38, 40 both, 41, 42, 43, 46,
46–47

Chicago Historical Society: 16
(Arthur Siegel, ICHi-26128)

© Bill Crofton: 31

© Frank Lloyd Wright
Archives: 35

Frank Lloyd Wright Home
and Studio Foundation:
1 (H&S 167)

© Farrell Grehan: 33, 34, 36

© Hedrich-Blessing:
18 (Scott McDonald);
20 (Nick Merrick)

© Balthazar Korab: 6–7, 8, 11,
12, 13, 37, 39, 48, 49, 50, 51,
53, 54–55, 55

© Steinkamp/Ballogg Chicago:
19 and 21 (James Stein-
kamp); 22 and 25 (George
Pfoertner); 28 and 32
(Mark Ballogg); 44 and 45
(James Steinkamp)

© John Thorpe: 27

. . . .